Parental drug and alcohol misuse

Resilience and transition among young people

Angus Bancroft, Sarah Wilson, Sarah Cunningham-Burley,
Kathryn Backett-Milburn and Hugh Masters

JR
JOSEPH
ROWNTREE
FOUNDATION

1904
2004

The **Joseph Rowntree Foundation** has supported this project as part of its programme of research and innovative development projects, which it hopes will be of value to policy makers, practitioners and service users. The facts presented and views expressed in this report are, however, those of the authors and not necessarily those of the Foundation.

Joseph Rowntree Foundation
The Homestead
40 Water End
York YO30 6WP
Website: www.jrf.org.uk

ISBN 1 85935 248 0   (paperback)
ISBN 1 85935 249 9   (pdf: available at www.jrf.org.uk)

A CIP catalogue record for this report is available from the British Library.

Cover design by Adkins Design

Prepared and printed by:
York Publishing Services Ltd
64 Hallfield Road
Layerthorpe
York YO31 7ZQ
Tel: 01904 430033; Fax: 01904 430868; Website: www.yps-publishing.co.uk

Further copies of this report, or any other JRF publication, can be obtained either from the JRF website (www.jrf.org.uk/bookshop/) or from our distributor, York Publishing Services Ltd, at the above address.

Contents

Acknowledgements

The research team would like to thank: the Joseph Rowntree Foundation, who funded the study, and in particular Susan Taylor and Marguerite Owen; Neil McKeganey of the Centre for Drug Misuse Research, University of Glasgow; the members of the Project Advisory Group, whose advice was constructive and helpful; Lothian Research Ethics Committee; Napier University; the University of Edinburgh; the many services that helped us find respondents; and, above all, the young people who took part and who gave generously of their time to discuss their experiences frankly and openly.

Glossary

We have used respondents' own terms when quoting them. However, some words may require explanation for non-Scottish readers.

Aboot:	About
Cannae:	Cannot
Couldnae:	Could not
Daen:	Doing
Dinnae:	Do not
Doesnae:	Does not
Fae:	From
Greet:	Cry
Havenae:	Have not
Heid:	Head
Highers:	Scottish secondary qualification
Ken:	Know
Mare:	More
Mind:	Remember
Oot:	Out
Stay:	Live
Tae:	To
Willnae:	Will not
Wouldnae:	Would not

Executive summary

A growing number of children are affected by parental substance misuse, and policy and practice increasingly recognise the need to tackle the problems that this causes. Currently, the needs of older children are less well known or addressed. This study explores the experiences of 38 young people, aged 15–27 years, who had at least one parent with a drug or alcohol problem. The research was conducted using in-depth qualitative interviews, incorporating a 'life grid', to examine what these young people reported about their childhoods, their current situation and their futures. Both men and women participated in the study, from diverse backgrounds. Participants were recruited through a range of formal and informal settings.

Key findings

- The young people's interview accounts portrayed disrupted and difficult lives. Parental substance misuse was at the centre of a web of problems that often included violence and neglect. The young people suggested that they only gradually recognised that there was a problem, and also that they then had to manage this knowledge both within the family and beyond. Uncertainty about reactions of others, concerns about stigma and types of interventions that might ensue from services all seemed to limit the sharing of their difficulties. A large minority had a drug problem themselves, and although we cannot say that this resulted directly from parental substance misuse, it was another source of vulnerability for them.

- Most respondents experienced considerable lack in a parent's capacity to provide practical and emotional care, although some made a distinction between being cared for and cared about, the latter suggesting a continued importance attached to a parental role despite enormous difficulties. About half of the respondents, mostly women, reported that they had had to take on parenting roles, caring for siblings and/or parents. In many ways, these young people experienced a foreshortened childhood, with early responsibilities for their own and others' care.

- Alcohol and drug misuse had some different impacts. Respondents with alcohol-misusing parents talked more about violence and parental 'disappearances' from the home. The short- and long-term effects of drugs on the parent's health could be more frightening, and the illegal nature of drugs meant that respondents felt more effort had to be put into concealment and silence.

- Nonetheless, respondents described a range of ways in which they managed to get by on a day-to-day basis within their difficult family environments, for example by removing themselves to a room for respite and safety. Respondents also described many different sources of, often informal, support, including helpful non-parental relationships. These could be with siblings, other relatives, neighbours, friends, teachers and service workers; however, these often proved fragile and conditional.

- Respondents also talked about their futures; many had already moved into independent accommodation, sometimes supported by services. All had similar goals and dreams in terms of getting a job and house and having a family. For some, especially those with a substance misuse problem, their focus was much more on the present and getting their lives together. For others, further or higher education was seen as a route to ensure current or future independence. However, the respondents' accounts suggest no smooth passages into adulthood, not least because their childhoods were themselves characterised by adult responsibilities and many changes and transitions.

Key policy and practice implications

- The complexity of the experiences that these young people reported suggest the need for integrated policy and service provision, extending from childhood into young adulthood. The problems described by these young people cross-cut policy areas, yet are often hidden from view.

- Disclosure of problems and sharing of information are far from straightforward and need to be handled sensitively, with the young person's own views and wishes taken seriously.

- Young people affected by parental substance misuse need to become part of debates about the kinds of supports they need and value. It is important to recognise their own agency and ability to manage adverse life circumstances and, where appropriate, to enhance the processes they themselves identified as helpful.

- Services can support children in a number of ways, both when living with the substance misuser and thereafter. For example, support is needed for children who care for adults and siblings. Young carers groups were especially appreciated by those that were involved in them. Non-stigmatising acknowledgement of their situation can help, together with informal, unobtrusive provision of support.

- As many of these young people were developing plans for their futures, and saw setting up independently as a positive step, youth-oriented services can assist this process. A less formal youth work approach seemed to be appreciated by many; an expansion of the profile of such services may help support these young people affected by parental substance misuse as they grow up.

- Public debates tend to emphasise drug misuse. The impact of alcohol misuse on children is less often acknowledged, an omission felt keenly by some of our respondents, especially in light of the association they perceived it to have with domestic violence.

1 Introduction

Background

It is estimated that there are 250–350,000 dependent children living with parental drug misuse (Advisory Council on the Misuse of Drugs, 2003) and 920,000 living with parental alcohol misuse (Alcohol Concern, 2000) in the UK. Parental substance misuse[1] can cause considerable harm. Children of substance misusers are at risk from emotional and physical neglect, and of developing serious emotional and social problems themselves later in life (Cuijpers *et al.*, 1999).

More needs to be known about the lives of children of substance misusers. Research and practice are focusing more and more on 'resilience', those aspects of the child's life, relationships and choices that protect them against risk (Gilligan, 2001). The processes contributing to risk and resilience in this population need to be examined. Older children (15 and over) are a less frequently studied group, their views are less often represented in policy debates on this issue, and there are fewer services for them. Understanding their needs and experiences is important. This period is a transitional one, where the young person is moving into adulthood and may be assessing the longer-term legacy of having a substance-using parent.

This study addressed some of these issues. It researched the experiences of older children (15–27 years) of substance-using parents. Its key aim was to explore their accounts of their childhoods, their pathways to independence and the daily practices which might constitute survival, coping or resilience. It examined: the situations they were in; the difficulties they encountered; what helped and the resources that were available to them; the choices they made; where they are now; and what they feel the future holds for them. Key questions addressed by the study are: what problems, both at the time and later, does parental substance misuse cause? What helps the young people get through these experiences? What can be done by services to help?

To address these questions, respondents' perceptions of risk and interpretations of the past, present and future impact of parental substance misuse were examined. The methods and processes of creating and sustaining resilience both in themselves and in their families were studied. Resilience was approached not as a fixed trait, nor as the ability to 'bounce back' against the odds, but as a series of choices made and strategies adopted by children to help them 'get by' in their lives. To facilitate this, family and peer relationships and relationships with service providers were explored. Relevant sociological factors were considered, including socio-economic circumstances, gender and other social contexts, and the impact of different forms of parental substance misuse. Throughout, the young people's own sense of agency has been placed at the centre of the research, which explores in detail their accounts of the decisions they made, the actions they took and the contexts surrounding them.

Study design and ethics

The study involved 38 young people who had experienced parental substance misuse for a substantial period in their childhoods, whether or not they felt they had been particularly affected by it. This is a hard-to-reach group who are partially unknown to services and not frequently visible in the research literature. The sample was recruited from a range of sources: community drug agencies; youth groups; young carers organisations; personal contacts; higher and further education institutions; and a drug maintenance clinic. The sample was designed to reflect a range of experiences and circumstances. It is intentionally diverse, including people from different social backgrounds, different regions of Scotland and contrasting family circumstances. The sample was purposively recruited to include male and female respondents, and a range of respondents whose parents had drug and alcohol problems, including those who experienced substance misuse by mothers and by fathers.

Special consideration was given to ethical requirements due to the nature of the sample population and the subject matter. Respondents read an information sheet outlining the study and signed one form consenting to be interviewed and another consenting to the interview being recorded. They were told that they could refuse to answer any questions and terminate the interview at any point, without having to give a reason. This was reinforced during the interview. In the case of recruitment from the drug maintenance clinic, ethical approval was sought and gained from the local health board research ethics committee. Parental consent was not required for those aged 16 and over. It was not sought for the one respondent who was under 16. He was judged by our researcher and the agency through which he was recruited to be competent in the terms of the Gillick ruling, and the interview took place in the protective environment of a support organisation fully aware of his family

circumstances. This was approved by the Project Advisory Group and by the agency involved.

Data collection consisted of qualitative interviews supported by a 'life grid' and an open-ended topic guide. They were conducted by Sarah Wilson. The life grid is a method for collecting biographical data. It helped the respondents to talk about what were often emotional past events and to provide a biographical context for discussions about the present. On the whole, respondents talked extensively about the topics raised and frequently expressed satisfaction at being given the opportunity to do so. All interviews were recorded and transcribed. Initial interpretive readings of the transcripts by the research team helped to form key themes for more detailed coding and analysis. Interview transcripts were then coded thematically by Sarah Wilson using NVivo.[2] They were analysed by code and demographic variable, and as whole interviews. Analysis was conducted by individual team members and conclusions drawn were then discussed by the team. The data were then reanalysed to confirm or explore these conclusions further.

The young people

The young people's experiences and current situations varied extensively. Twenty respondents were women, 18 were men. Although they ranged in age from 15 to 27, most (23) were aged 16 to 19. Respondents had lived in a variety of communities, some rural, a few affluent, but mostly urban and deprived. Most came from lower social class backgrounds, and most were in work-poor households. Six were from middle-class families.[3] Many respondents reported a history of mental health problems: one had been sectioned[4] for a time. A few had criminal careers, one of which was very extensive, involving periods in custody from age 16. None were members of an ethnic minority.

Their parents[5] used alcohol and a variety of mostly street, but occasionally prescription, drugs, as illustrated in Table 1.

Around half of the respondents engaged in very little if any substance misuse. Some were heavy alcohol and drug users themselves, and more had been so in the past. Twelve were current or past heroin users and, of these, eight were currently part of a methadone maintenance programme. Twenty were using or had used cannabis, and nine ecstasy. Three described themselves as heavy cannabis users. One heavily self-medicated for depression using ecstasy. Other drugs used included speed, valium, acid, magic mushrooms, dihydrocodeine, GHB ('liquid ecstasy'), cocaine and nail varnish. One respondent described himself as being a heavy drinker currently, with a further six saying they had been heavy drinkers in the past.

Of those respondents who had developed problems with drugs or alcohol as teenagers, several had stopped or had controlled their use of these drugs by the time of the interview. One respondent was introduced to heroin by her parents, while another had obtained heroin by stealing it from his parents. A small minority had used cannabis or drunk with their parents. Looking back, some respondents criticised this as having legitimated the misuse of harder drugs. However, the route most respondents cited as the way they had started to take opiates,

Table 1 Substance misuse by respondents' parents

Alcohol: 22	Ten respondents had fathers who were alcohol misusers, and also the cousin of one of these used heroin. Seven respondents had mothers who were alcohol misusers, one of whom also used cannabis. Four respondents had both parents who were alcohol misusers, and one of these had two foster-fathers who were alcohol misusers. One had a grandfather in a parental role who was an alcohol misuser.
Drugs: 11	Five had fathers who were drug misusers, of whom three used heroin and two cannabis. Three had mothers who were drug misusers, of whom one used heroin and amphetamines, one used dihydrocodeine and one used cannabis. Two had both parents who were drug misusers, all heroin users. One had a heroin-using brother in a parental role. It was notable that heavy cannabis use could on its own be a serious problem for children.
Polysubstance (drugs and alcohol): 5	One had a father who was a polysubstance misuser, two had mothers, and two had both parents. Substances used along with alcohol included heroin, dihydrocodeine, poppers, valium, amphetamines, cannabis and glue.

as well as other drugs, including cocaine, amphetamines and ecstasy, was through their friends rather than their parents.

> *I've no had a settled life.*
> (Paul, 25, stepmother and two foster-fathers alcohol misusers)

Some respondents lived on their own, several lived in supported accommodation, and some stayed with partners, friends and parents. A history of disruption was common to most of their lives. Some had been in local authority care and foster care, and some had been homeless. One man had been in 13 foster homes from the age of 12, and then in eight different children's homes. Their family structures were often complex. Brothers and sisters might live with a separated parent. Some had very unstable family histories, and many had experienced parental separation and repartnering.

All the respondents had been through very painful experiences, although at the time of interview they mostly were no longer living with the substance-using parent. The language they used to describe their experiences often seemed very understated in comparison to the subject matter. They rarely expressed anger or became upset in interviews, even when describing the most harrowing behaviour by parents. Many, though not all, had used or were

using different types of support services. These provided an opportunity to talk in depth about their past, and the narratives some told seemed to draw on these discussions, but much of what was said came from reflection on their situation and that of others in their peer group:

> *So there was four o' us* [friends] *right? We all got brought up in the same school in the same area. But I was the one wi' the alcoholic parents. And when I think about it they three have a decent job, a car and a house and a mortgage and I've no. You know. Is that a direct result of what I've been through. I dunno. You don't know do you?*
> (Ian, 23, mother and father alcohol misusers)

Conclusion

The narratives collected in this study provide an overview of respondents' pasts, a snapshot of their present, and a window onto their futures. In their accounts, parental substance misuse was often tied up with other issues, such as poverty, family and home disruption, violence, and their own substance misuse. The sample had diverse experiences and came from a variety of backgrounds. Despite differences, which will be highlighted as appropriate in the following chapters, there was also striking similarity in their accounts of their lives and the ways in which they dealt with their difficulties.

2 Living with parental substance misuse

This chapter examines the extent, nature and contexts of parental substance misuse, and goes on to look closely at the impact respondents said it had on their lives over time. It involved significant disruption and neglect and had a profound effect on the quality of family relationships and on roles within the family. Unpredictability was a theme running through their accounts. Many respondents said that they had to take on parenting roles, caring for siblings and/or parents. Several had been 'looked after' at times, either in foster care or by grandparents, aunts or other relatives.

Recognition and reaction

In some families, parents were reported to have had substance misuse problems since before the respondents' birth or since they were very young. In others, parental substance misuse developed later and represented an important change. This was reflected in the young people's accounts of how they became aware of their parents' substance misuse problems. Twelve of the respondents did not or could not pinpoint the age when they became aware of it. Awareness of the signs of substance misuse seemed to be separate from knowing there was a problem. They reported becoming aware of the signs between five and 14 years old. There was often a progressive awareness of there being a problem, which ultimately led to recognition that their parents' behaviour was 'not normal':

> Just a, I mean just a normal, I was brought up. I didnae really think anything bad o' it. Because I didnae, I was just used tae it eh? I was just used tae being roond everything.
> (Dan, 21, mother and two stepfathers heroin misusers)

Recognising certain types of drug misuse especially required a frame of reference. One man was aware of his mother's cannabis misuse from a young age and at age 11 associated the tinfoil he kept finding around the house with it, rather than as evidence of a heroin habit. Aged 13, he was no longer so sure:

> It gradually built up and I was aboot thirteen when she started getting intae it heavy and that's when I realised it was smack. Because it was just ... I just thought it was hash when I was eleven eh.
> (Dan, 21, mother and two stepfathers heroin misusers)

Only two respondents reported being directly told of a parent's substance misuse, and in both cases this was by the non-using parent. Others overheard family members discussing it. Awareness was much sharper when substance misuse and associated difficulties reflected a sudden change in circumstances. This was the case for about half of the respondents. Their accounts illustrated the connections between parental substance misuse and various other sources of family stress, including: repartnering, where the new partner had a substance misuse problem; a parent's grief at bereavement; a parent's reaction to revelations of sexual abuse of another child; and the development of problems after suffering a work-related injury.

Respondents in this group could often remember these events more clearly, even when younger. Several made a clear distinction between an, albeit idealised, 'before' and 'after' period. For this woman, everything changed when she was 14:

That's when like my dad got the jail and then my mum went kind of off the rails ... But everything was fine till I was aboot 14 ... We had a brilliant life, we were really happy aye. Because we were never without anything.
(Emma, 21, mother alcohol misuser)

For two respondents, parents' substance misuse was associated with the young person's own misuse. Stuart (19, mother cannabis misuser) reported that his mother started using hash soon after he did at the age of 11. Similarly, Nicole's (20, mother heroin and amphetamines misuser) mother started to misuse heroin (in addition to other drugs) after Nicole herself started as a teenager.

Patterns of substance misuse, unpredictability and relapse

Most respondents described their parents' substance misuse as 'constant', apart from a few attempts to give up, or as defined by a predictable pattern. For example, some said that their parents only drank at night (and most of the night) after work. Tabetha (17, mother alcohol misuser) described how her mother would drink on five days a week but on two days she would stay inside the house, clean and drink coffee in an effort to restrict her drinking.

For a significant minority, parental substance misuse was relatively unpredictable. One man described binges lasting a few months interspersed with periods of 'normality', which he loved:

Oh it was great, when they were sober it was great. I used to love it, you know, I could sit in the hoose and go through and my dinner would be ready. And it would just be like a normal life ... I

could take my pals up and go how you doing, come in. And sit wi' them and watch the telly and be quiet at night and go to sleep nae bother. And you came hame fae school the next day and you'd know right away. It takes ages to answer the door, the door disnae answer. Because it's the same routine for years ... You know they're oot drunk.
(Ian, 23, mother and father alcohol misusers)

A few respondents reported that their parents had stopped their substance misuse over the last few years. A more frequent narrative in these interviews, however, related to the sense of let-down experienced by many respondents when the parent had tried to give up their substance misuse, but had then relapsed. Several respondents recounted how they had learnt to protect themselves by not trusting that the parent would remain abstinent and preparing for the use to start again.

Not all respondents preferred their parents to be drug free, however. This man, for example, felt that it would make his life easier if his father cut down on his cannabis misuse, rather than giving it up altogether:

Sarah Wilson: *Has he ever tried to give up before?*

Adam: *He's tried it before but it's like ... But when he stops altogether it's usually heavy moaning and he's always in the biggest moans and moods. He never stops moaning. So sometimes. It's alright if he's on it, but no so heavy.*
(Adam, 16, father cannabis misuser)

Impact of substance misuse

A minority of respondents did not perceive parental substance misuse to be the most formative influence on their lives. For them, having a parent with a mental health problem or other illness or having been sexually abused was more important. For the majority, however, parental substance misuse was a key element in their accounts of their lives as they were growing up, affecting their relationships with their parents as well as the dynamics, roles and positions within the family.

> I'll tell you something right see living wi' two alcoholic parents fer the amount of time I did. It was the most hellish experience that you could ever imagine.
>
> (Ian, 23, mother and father alcohol misusers)

Respondents seemed to have low expectations of parents and parenting, with a few saying they thought that their substance-using parent had done a good job. As this woman put it:

> No he's like my ma like, I'll gi' her her due she always like me and my wee brother never wanted fer nothing ... we were never like ken just left.
>
> (Louise, 18, mother heroin misuser)

Most qualified these positive appraisals of their parenting, however. Tabetha, for example, immediately mentioned her mother's aggression. One man raised the financial problems caused by his mother's heavy cannabis misuse:

> When I was about 15, she was smoking ... £105 a week it was costing her. She was only getting £115 in benefits.
>
> (Stuart, 19, mother cannabis misuser)

Overall, a large majority of respondents thought that their substance-misusing parent had not looked after their basic needs. Many reported that from an early age they had taken responsibility for their own cleaning, cooking and shopping. This woman highlighted how surprised she was that her foster-family changed the sheets regularly, recalling that her parents' house:

> Julia: Was like a squat really so I would ... well tidying was a bit difficult but ... me and my brother would try and washing, just doing things like that, cooking ...
>
> SW: So how old were you when you started cooking things?
>
> Julia: Ehm, I don't know, maybe about 10.
>
> (Julia, 16, mother and father alcohol misusers)

Michael (19, father alcohol misuser) showed the interviewer the scars he had sustained from burning himself on a cooking ring at the age of eight. His father had been asleep drunk on the sofa at the time, and he had had to call his grandmother to take him to hospital. Several other respondents also reported that their parents' substance misuse had put them or their siblings at physical risk, for example from fires caused by dropped cigarette butts and leaving electrical appliances on.

A common theme to many interviews was the violence, and other forms of abuse, meted out by parents. Twenty respondents spoke about physical abuse or cruelty; 12 (including five not included in the first group) spoke about verbal abuse and humiliation. Three raised issues of sexual abuse. Many of these accounts were, of course, harrowing:

My dad was injecting, that eh and he used tae batter my mum. He used tae batter me. My brother, it was just at the time me and my wee brother, and we used tae get battered. And there was a time my dad battered me and battered my mum and I actually took tae go to court ... But I cannae remember because when I was younger my dad was intae drugs and he used tae beat us. He used tae batter us, beat us up, whatever you want tae call it.
(Claire, 22, father heroin misuser)

Fourteen respondents, like Claire above, spoke of constant domestic violence, carried out by men in all but one case. It seemed that many had grown up in homes characterised by fear and dread. This man's experience was not unusual:

The whole atmosphere in the house would change ... My sisters would never come oot their rooms ... Eh, my mum always used to be sitting on the edge of her seat like waiting for him to come home.
(Robbie, 18, stepfather alcohol misuser)

In most cases, the respondents associated parents' violence or increased violence with substance misuse, and particularly alcohol. Only three of the respondents who reported physical abuse had parents who did not misuse alcohol. For several respondents, this was an important reason why they felt that alcohol misuse should be considered on a par with or as more serious than most drug misuse.

One man's consideration of whether or not he should have hit his father to protect his mother provides an insight into a world in which not responding to his father's violence had immediate consequences for his mother:

But then again where does the limit stop. What you can do to protect your family? You know, should I have hit my dad? I think I should because eh when I was peeling him off he was just going back and back. So I decided, well, I'm gonna have to hit him a couple of times and hopefully that'll stop him ... Never did you know.
(Ian, 23, mother and father alcohol misusers)

Absences, emotions and relationships

Parental absences were also raised as problematic. Two respondents spoke about the fear and uncertainty associated with parents disappearing for long periods:

And she never came home for four days. And I had like, I had to cook and clean ... and put my sister oot to school. Get her up. Em, and then it just got worse and worse fae there. Like I used to have to phone hospitals and stuff and police stations because she wouldnae leave notes at times. And she'd just disappear and I was always scared in case she was ... lying somewhere, dead or something.
(Emma, 21, mother alcohol misuser)

A small minority of respondents' parents had been sent to prison. In the majority of these cases, however, this was seen as preferable to the parent being at home, as it allowed some respite:

Sarah Wilson:	*So was he ever in prison when you were living with your gran?*
Sean:	*Mm.*
SW:	*So did that leave you alone with your gran? What was that like?*
Sean:	*A wee bit quieter.*

SW: *So you preferred that?*

Sean: *Aye. I used tae like it when he was away* [laughs].
(Sean, 17, father cannabis misuser)

The ultimate parental absence was when respondents were placed in foster care or children's homes. This was the case for eight respondents, three of whom had experienced a long list of placements in foster homes, children's homes and secure units. While some of these respondents had come to appreciate this care, Paul (25, stepmother and two foster-fathers alcohol misusers) referred to the 'stigma' of being in care as the most difficult aspect of his life.

Respondents often commented on the quality of their relationships with their parents. This relationship was clearly important to them, but the interviews raised difficulties relating to communication with their parents around substance misuse, as well as more generally (see Chapter 3). Several criticised their parents' inability to show consistent interest in their lives, something often described as 'not being there' for them. Dan (21, mother and two stepfathers heroin misusers) felt that his mother just did not 'hear' her children's emotions. Another man related:

It's like him, if I went home tonight I would go in and sit in the living room ... if my mum was in her bed ... put on the telly. [And] he'll be sitting ... having a smoke. And he willnae say anything, he'll just sit and change the channel, or go 'that's alright', just kinda usual, small chat. Then he'll go 'right, I'm going to bed'. And that's about it ... he disnae really ask me how I'm daen or how's my day or anything like that.
(Adam, 16, father cannabis misuser)

Blurring of roles and child carers

Problems with parenting led to a greater or lesser degree of role reversal for about half of the respondents. Nineteen respondents described how they looked after the practical or emotional needs of their parents or siblings. For this woman and several other respondents, the role reversal was clear:

That was the case, just it was like I was the mum and she was like the child.
(Rachel, 17, mother alcohol misuser)

She felt she had had to look after her mother '24/7', shopping, cooking, cleaning for her, and running her baths when she had not washed. This was also observed in others:

Because there's my brother's girlfriend right, she was taking smack eh ... And her wee daughter was looking after her and she was, when she was taking it eh. And she was like 'that's my mum' and that.
(Craig, 21, brother heroin misuser in a parental role)

One woman was also concerned about her father's physical condition:

I'm scared, I'm always scared in case he's sick in his sleep or something. So I'm always, whenever he falls asleep I'm always turning him over and all that.
(Kate, 16, father alcohol misuser)

Several respondents also recounted the ways in which they had looked after the practical needs of their younger siblings, and sometimes tried to protect them from violence. The responsibility and motivation were with the child: they reported that they simply had assumed responsibility because parents were incapable.

Several described their parents as emotionally dependent on them. Their accounts suggested that some parents thought of their relationship with their children as something like a friendship. This woman described how her mother would wake her at night, just to talk or argue with someone:

> She'll come in and wake me up because she needs somebody to talk tae and that. It's no the fact that she's like needing somebody tae talk tae. I mean I'll talk to my mum if she needs anything but that's like I could be up for college early in the morning. And she wakes us up like late at night.
> (Tabetha, 17, mother alcohol misuser)

Overall, respondents had conflicting feelings about their role as carers. One woman felt she had been a substitute mother for her younger siblings. Her mother had recently stopped drinking, and previously stopped all drug misuse, but she found it difficult to relinquish this role:

> It's like I'm used tae daen all the tidying and the cooking and like telling [siblings] when tae be in and who no tae hang about with and who no, where no to go ... And my mum's started daen that and ... it's like a kind of conflict between us now because she's like saying 'you're 17, I'm the mum'.
> (Alexis, 17, mother alcohol, heroin, poppers misuser)

Another woman spoke of similar difficulties in moving away from this role after so many years. Although very difficult, caring for her mother had given her an approved role in the eyes of her neighbours and the local shopkeeper:

> When I was looking after my mum, I was looked ... up at. People really did think the world of me because I was young and I was looking after my mum.
> (Rachel, 17, mother alcohol misuser)

Trying to move away from home to 'live her own life' required, as she termed it, a determination to 'break the chains' linking her to her mother. For several respondents, the family dynamics around caring for others were very powerful and difficult to resist, particularly, it seemed, for young women. Rachel, for example, had several older brothers, none of whom had felt they should have to care for their mother. Several respondents reported guilt at no longer being in a position to care for parents once they had left home. With hindsight, however, several were angry at the hard work and loss of childhood their caring had entailed, a point developed further in Chapter 4:

> I shouldnae have had to grow up like that. I wouldnae say I grew up ... I would say I've been dragged up because I had to do all that.
> (Emma, 21, mother alcohol misuser)

Gender and socio-economic status

There were gendered processes and experiences underlying respondents' accounts of their family lives. They reported that the experience of living with a substance-using mother was different to the experience of living with a substance-using father. Of course, this may relate to gendered expectations about parenting roles, or the fact that more of the young people grew up in lone-mother households, and that it was often the mother who was the single continuous carer in their lives.

Violence and abuse were reported as more common amongst male parents. It was mostly, though not entirely, committed by fathers and stepfathers towards children or female partners. Rejection of fathers seemed to be more absolute than of mothers, especially where violence and abuse were involved, although this could reflect the greater likelihood of the father being absent. Stigma also seemed to be a gendered experience, with the embarrassment or shame of having a drug-misusing mother reported as being especially acutely felt:

> Because when people see her in the street and she's out her head and that. That embarrasses me, people thinking, well, 'his mum's a junkie', you know. Because they're like that.
> (Graham, 18, mother dihydrocodeine misuser)

Non-using mothers could have a burden of care and responsibility that the using father did not. For some, fathers were expected to provide both resources for the family and authority within it. Substance misuse could lead to role reversal between parents, with the mother expected to take up both an authority and a providing role. Their doing this was not always respected by children. For Kate (16, father alcohol misuser), her father was a very important part of her life. It was her non-using mother whom she was harsher on, because her mother was the 'more serious person' and the authority figure. She still did housework because her mum was working, and saw it as on a par with doing the same for her dad when he was drunk: '[Housework] was mostly with my dad. I still have to do it with my mum … because my mum's working'.

For some, if the mother was the non-using parent it seemed that she had to help the respondent deal with the using parent in order to show that she cared for them. For this man, his mother did not stand up for him with his stepfather:

> Because my mum doesn't seem to care anymore for me. Well she cares aboot me obviously. But like when [stepfather] says something, my mum just agrees wi' him. She disnae say anything aboot me.
> (Brian, 16, stepfather alcohol, cousin heroin misusers)

There seemed to be an expectation that the role of the mother was to be 'strong' with a using parent. The expectations on the mother to protect were partly because she was often the one in a position to do this, and some respondents acknowledged that mothers – both users and non-users – tried hard to 'make things normal'.

With mothers who were users, there was sometimes a sense of responsibility on the part of the child. Graham (18, mother dihydrocodeine misuser) felt closer to his father but moved in with his mother to help her. 'Losing a mother' to drugs seemed to happen in a different way to losing her to alcohol. The start of a mother's drug use was sometimes associated with a particular boyfriend or stepfather who was held responsible for it:

> Louise: Probably 'cause my stepdad was daen it or something.
>
> Sarah Wilson: Did she [mother] use drugs before him?
>
> Louise: Nuh.
>
> SW: Okay. And what do you think she gets out of it?

Louise: *Fae using drugs?*

SW: *Yeah.*

Louise: *Stopped her being sare and everything because like, I dunno.*

SW: *Stops her from being sad?*

Louise: *Sore.*

SW: *Sore. Why is she sore?*

Louise: *'Cause she, you get a habit and it makes you taking it 'cause you're sore.*
            (Louise, 18, mother heroin misuser)

Then, respondents were more likely to see their mothers as victims, and felt strongly about this. Conflict could arise, and sons in particular felt rejected if the mother stuck with a drug-using boyfriend. Mothers were more likely to go on 'benders', usually alcohol induced, and disappear for long periods of time (weeks in some cases) with children being left to fend for themselves. However, this may simply reflect the fact that these mothers were lone parents, and that if the father disappeared it would not have had such an impact.

Socio-economic status appeared to shape the impact of substance misuse. This woman's parents had lost their jobs due to alcoholism but retained the accoutrements of a middle-class lifestyle, such as living in a wealthy area, partly due to loans and transfers from relatives:

Because em, they [parents] have huge financial problems at the moment because they've got a huge debt from the house that ... because they haven't been paying it off, they've been spending it on drink and stuff, so they can, they've got like, they had to sell the house and like whatever money was left over, like there wasn't any money left over from the debt. So my grandparents had to buy them a new flat and stuff.
(Julia, 16, mother and father alcohol misusers)

Some respondents had resources transferred to them from their extended family. Substance misuse had interfered with parents' ability to work. Drug misuse was strongly associated with criminal activity as some drug-using parents supported their habit through dealing. One mother had been a relatively successful dealer in financial terms, although after being convicted most of the wealth she accumulated was taken as the proceeds of crime.

Drugs and alcohol

The respondents' accounts suggest that there were some differences between parental drug and alcohol use, although overall it was striking how similar the accounts of respondents with drug, alcohol and polysubstance-misusing parents were. Drugs had the effect of producing indifference and distance in the parent. Alcohol tended to make them more invasive, either in a violent or maudlin way, and was associated with parents angrily 'flaring up' verbally or physically. In this sample, violence was, in respondents' accounts, strongly associated with alcohol, and sexual abuse with volatile substance misuse.

Parents were reported as often wanting to discuss their own emotional issues with their child when they had been drinking heavily. Some respondents also spoke about emotional blackmail by their alcohol-misusing parents, often in the form of suicide threats. Drunken declarations of love and caring were resented as meaningless:

Back fae the pub, that's when he gives you all his loveydovey stories. 'Oh I love you', 'you're my bairn', 'dinnae ken what I'd do without you'. But he doesn't say nothing like that when he's sober … Makes you think, 'well what's the point in saying it when you're drunk if you cannae say it when you're sober?'
(Lana, 20, father alcohol misuser)

Parents were mentioned as more likely to damage themselves when drunk. Alcohol could be a big problem on public or convivial occasions, such as a parents evening or a Christmas celebration. Alcohol misusers, usually fathers, seemed to place more store on reciprocity. Lana (20, father alcohol misuser) had nowhere else to go and moved back in with her father for a short time: 'He sorta agreed he'll help me if I can help him, ken, get off the drink.' This did not work: 'It was just an excuse to get somebody else back in the house.'

In instances of polysubstance misuse, the 'dominant substance' in terms of the effect on the respondents' lives was often alcohol, although this was usually in cases where the drug was dihydrocodeine, valium or cannabis rather than heroin. The experiences of children of polysubstance misusers highlighted a key difference between drugs and alcohol: that alcohol would often take the parent out of the home, for example to the pub or on benders for several days or weeks, and separate them from their child. With drugs, the parents would be absent at home, meaning that when they were high they would be there but 'not there'.

Well. When she was taking drugs, my mum was there, but she wasnae all there if you know what I mean.
(Graham, 18, mother dihydrocodeine misuser)

The illegality of drugs added an extra layer of worry, especially if the user was in debt to dealers:

No want to see him getting killed or that fer the money … he's got twelve grand over his heid man.
(Craig, 21, brother heroin misuser in a parental role)

Illegality was sometimes accepted as normal, but even then children were aware that they had to be complicit in concealing parents' use. Dan (21, mother and two stepfathers heroin misusers) was aware of the implicit rules about what could be said: 'if they [police] ever ask you anything and that just say nothing'.

Among respondents, there was often acute embarrassment and, in some cases, shame at their parents' behaviour. This was sometimes more acute with drug misuse, and, as noted above, with mothers more than with fathers:

I don't know. I'd just rather she [mother] drank … Because people wouldnae call her a junkie.
(Graham, 18, mother dihydrocodeine misuser)

The meaning of family

All of our sample said that they thought close family relationships, particularly those with parents and siblings, were important, even if this was demonstrated by the bitter reflection of a minority that they had not had this at all, or only partially, in their upbringing. Michael (19, father alcohol misuser) said, 'my pals are my family'. Most expressed expectations of parents that had often not been fulfilled. In spite of this, almost all said that they retained some closeness to, usually, one of their parents, sometimes the substance misuser. Their 'family' then retained both a symbolic and practical significance as relationships floundered, ended or were reformed.

Like most young people, our respondents expected parents to be there for them unconditionally, to protect them, and to care for and about them. This expressed need for giving and receiving love permeated the interviews. They often wanted to love their parents, despite everything, and complete rejection of a parent seemed to be very hard and was quite unusual. One man said:

> In time right, maybe when I move to [the Highlands] after a few years I'll forgive them. Absence makes the heart grow fonder and all that crap. But I keep reminding myself, no I cannae forgive them because they did put me through absolute hell every single day of the week. It was twenty-four hours as well, you know.
> (Ian, 23, mother and father alcohol misusers)

But later he said that:

> Obviously I still go doon to my mum and dad's right. [Sarah Wilson: Aha] Because it's your mum and dad, you know, and it's just a built-in emotion I suppose isn't it?

Some were still holding on to the hope of change in their parents' behaviour. One man, who had not been in contact with his mother for some months after he had given her an ultimatum to quit using and leave her boyfriend, nevertheless said:

> [Sighs] Well hopefully, all I can say is that I hope she phones me and tells me that she's off drugs and away from her boyfriend, and then I'd be

right back down to see her but until then. [SW: You're not going to] I'll be waiting.
> (Graham, 18, mother dihydrocodeine misuser)

Many respondents spoke of feeling both angry at and sorry for their substance-misusing parent and of having some understanding of their behaviour. The latter was particularly the case among young people who had subsequently developed a heroin problem themselves. It was the few who had felt abandoned, abused or simply not cared about who expressed little hesitation about rejecting their parent.

Conclusion

Parental substance misuse impacts on children's lives in many ways. Its effects are shaped by factors such as the relationship with parents, gender, and the nature of the substance misuse. The harshest words from respondents were reserved for those parents who had, in their eyes, reneged on the basic expectations of loving and caring, whether they were the substance-misusing parent or not. Our interviews suggested that being a substance-misusing parent seemed to be something that, if not ever accepted, could nevertheless be made sense of. Respondents expressed mixed emotions of anger and feeling sorry for their substance-misusing parent. Despite enormous difficulties, family relationships, whether with parents or siblings, were described as continually important and many respondents had themselves had direct experience of caring for and about their family members.

3 What helps? What hurts? Managing and getting by

Focusing mostly on respondents' accounts of their lives before the age of 16, this chapter explores the resources and strategies that they developed and relied on throughout difficult experiences associated with their parents' substance misuse. It locates the help they were able to draw on from many sources, what they did, who they turned to, and how they 'got by'. It has long been noted by those working in child welfare that children exposed to similar risky experiences have a variety of outcomes. Some appear to slough off the hurt done to them and have positive outcomes. The concept of 'resilience' was developed to describe these children, and the qualities and factors that contributed to their apparent lack of vulnerability. A concern with promoting resilience has characterised work predominantly in psychology, social policy and child welfare (Gilligan, 2001; 2003).

Whilst resilience is seen as having its roots in childhood, it is important to understand it not as a fixed attribute, but as one that can change and be developed through experience. The data presented here are poignant, illustrating that 'getting by' and 'managing' are just that, day-to-day strategies of difficult childhoods. The analysis in this chapter begins to unpack the processes of resilience, how children learn to survive adverse circumstances and what helps them do so.

Challenging and taking control

One aspect of the role reversal discussed in the previous chapter was that respondents challenged the parent or attempted to assert control over their substance misuse, confronting the parent about their habit or trying to remove substances from them. Attempts to do so were reported to have taken place earlier in their lives, and were described somewhat hopelessly with hindsight by almost all. By the mid-teenage years, most seemed to have given up thinking they might be able to do anything to control their parents' substance misuse. Alexis (17, mother alcohol, heroin, poppers misuser), for example, had tried to limit her mother's alcohol misuse by controlling the family budget. She said she later abandoned this strategy as her mother would then buy alcohol on tab and she would have to pay off the resultant debts anyway.

Challenging their parents' substance misuse often seemed futile in the light of their parents' inability to accept that there was a problem.

> Em, me and my pals had a talk aboot it, you know, my best mate, he says, 'why do you no try and take your ma away fae it, ken? Hijack her and that. And take her away and everything tae your gran's and that?' But it was basically, she wasnae up fae daen it. She wasn't, ken, somebody's got tae want tae dae it – tae stop them daen it eh. So if she didnae want tae stop so there was nae point in trying tae get her tae stop if she didnae want tae stop eh.
> (Dan, 21, mother and two stepfathers heroin misusers)

One man said initially that he had never tried to stop his father smoking hash; indeed one of the only ways to get his father to do anything for him was by colluding and supporting the habit. He then recalled:

I've done, shouted at him about it before. But he just, doesn't take much attention in it ... and comes up with the excuse that it's because of his back.
(Adam, 16, father cannabis misuser)

Trial and error showed how this strategy could be harmful. For many, the consequences of trying to challenge or get rid of substances were rows, and often violence:

And he was that, 'where's my bag o' kit?' and a' that eh. And I says, 'It's doon the toilet.' And he says, 'Right. I'm gonna batter,' he battered me fer daen it and a' that.
(Craig, 21, brother heroin misuser in a parental role)

In addition, there was a sense that the parent could be put at risk by having their dependence disrupted.

A more reliable method of asserting control was to gain control over their environment, to find space over which they had control, or to leave. Nearly all respondents described how, when possible, they removed themselves physically from their parent. A few simply said that they went out and wandered about. However, for much of the time, particularly when younger, there was little option but to find ways of dealing with the situation within the home. Most often they removed themselves from the situation by going to their own room, often with siblings whom they were protecting or being protected by. Sometimes they put music on to drown out noise, read or watched TV, cried, or vented their feelings in other ways. One woman said that once she was old enough, she tried to go to friends' houses. Before this she would:

Just sit in my bedroom or watch TV or listen to music. And greet all the time and I was just so sad.
(Lucy, 17, mother alcohol misuser)

Mark (17, grandfather alcohol misuser) gave a vivid account of running away from his violent, alcohol-dependent grandfather and hiding or barricading himself into rooms in the house. This woman said she was often prevented from leaving the house by her alcohol-dependent parents, and described how she made use of the space afforded by their large house:

I read quite a lot and painted, like in my room if I got the chance and I'd tidy quite a lot ... On the weekend like after school I'd be like, 'Great, this is my mission, I want to tidy the house,' and stuff. But ... like I'd start doing it and then I just went oh no this is hopeless. Like you'd just see someone like drop a can or something like that and you're going upstairs tidying.
(Julia, 16, mother and father alcohol misusers)

In some cases, friends and a few neighbours had provided respite and escape routes, for example neighbours providing a place to go for food. Our interviews indicated that, as the respondents got older, they could go out with friends, getting away from the house, and some friends (and friends' parents) would allow them to stay overnight. Emma (21, mother alcohol misuser) was able to turn up at (older) friends' houses at 3 a.m. to avoid her mother's violence. These shelters were invaluable in giving respondents a safe place and a sense that they were not entirely isolated and exposed.

Parents: caring for and caring about

As was described in the previous chapter, respondents recounted a serious reduction in parenting capacity in the substance-using parent. However, 'support' from the parent did not just consist of practical care. A sense that the parent cared *about* them was important to respondents, even when the parent could not care *for* them. If this sense of being cared about was not present, a few respondents seemed to reject the substance-using parent. Rejecting that person could be part of limiting the hurt caused by them, as well as possibly providing some sense of control. Several made strong statements that they 'hated' this parent and would prefer never to see them again. As one man put it:

I went into care and ... he dinnae even bother to fucking phone me or fuck all. So I just tell him to fuck off.
(Michael, 19, father alcohol misuser)

Others had written the substance-using parent off:

My dad's a druggie, ken ... it's the way he is now, eh, he's decided.
(Tom, 22, and Peter, 25, fathers heroin misusers)

The roles and behaviours of step-parents were even more harshly judged if they had been the substance misuser. Robbie (18, stepfather alcohol misuser) had drawn some satisfaction from beating up his violent stepfather. Jane (19, stepfather alcohol misuser) had taken her stepfather's surname when she was younger, but had now rejected it because of his behaviour:

And I took his name at one stage so it was really like my dad but ... I wasn't and it was wrong and he'd really ... hurt me a lot.

Previous research has emphasised the potential importance of the 'other' (non-using) parent:

Just one, just as long as one person can, one parent can hold it together I think is the main thing.
(Jemma, 22, father heroin misuser)

For nine of these respondents, however, there was no 'other' parent, either because that parent also had a substance misuse problem, was in prison, had never been present, or, more frequently, had left when the respondent was very young. Several more respondents reported little or no care from their 'other' parent(s) when they were there. As stated in the previous chapter, non-using parents had to *show* they cared, and often were seen to fail, or be unable, to do this. If they could do so, however, it was warmly appreciated:

My mum used to protect me ... She'd be like 'right just go up to your room and pretend you're sleeping' ... She said she'll have a word with him and try and calm him down ... And I'd hear my mum screaming at night as well. When he used to hit her.
(Robbie, 18, stepfather alcohol misuser)

Parents who lived away from the home could also provide havens and respites. One man said he had been closest to his father over the years. His dad was particularly important to him because not only did he currently provide a haven for a half-sibling from the substance-misusing mother but he had also:

Stood by me through everything. Everything. He's ... always been there for me. Even though I got put in a home and I did feel deserted and all that, I

know now that my dad didnae want me to get put in the home, that my dad tried to stop it.
(Graham, 18, mother dihydrocodeine misuser)

Supportive family relationships

Inside and outside the home, respondents found many supportive relationships: brothers and sisters, grandparents, aunts and uncles, neighbours and others. When they were so isolated that they did not have these, and had no sense that anyone cared about them, their situation became especially bleak.

The sense of being 'looked out for' by at least one parent helped respondents get through life with a substance-using parent. Siblings could also look out for them, but also needed looking out for.

I tried to keep [younger sister] *out of the way. I kept her in the bedroom, put a video on and things like that.*
(Nikki, 19, mother amphetamines, stepfather glue misusers)

Support for and from siblings was important to some respondents, but its existence could not be assumed. As a result of parental separation and having been separated in foster care, ten respondents had had little or no contact with most or all of their siblings. Several others reported that they had not been close to siblings for long periods, as they did not agree with siblings' responses to their parents' substance misuse. For example, although very close to her older sister now, this woman had not appreciated her sister's attempts to confront their father about his drinking while they still lived together:

She pushed the boundary a wee bit … like one time … he was cooking the barbecue. And he was quite drunk … And she comes home and the neighbours are out in the other back gardens. So she calls him an alcoholic … and he went for her. And like … it was a nice day, we were having fun. Do you know what I mean? … I just lost a lot of respect for her.
(Ellie, 19, father alcohol misuser)

Some said they now felt isolated from other siblings through their different experiences and, in particular, by being treated worse than other siblings. Sophie (19, father alcohol misuser) felt like the family outcast. She was the only one who had been sexually abused by their father.

Nonetheless, several respondents reported very close, supportive sibling relationships. Such relationships could develop out of protective feelings towards younger siblings whom they tried to shield from their parents. Two named younger siblings as the person to whom they were closest. Another two described sharing the painful experiences and distress with their siblings, by crying or hiding together. Graham (18, mother dihydrocodeine misuser) had advised his younger half-brother to get out of the house as much as possible, away from their drug-abusing mother and her violent boyfriend, and to stay with his own father. This man had found his relationship with his mother improved after moving in with his sister:

Sarah Wilson: *What's been the best things for you so far?*

Ricky: *Em, staying at my big sister's has been like a lot better … And I still see my mum and stuff eh but I don't, things arnie like as they were. It's more relaxed.*
(Ricky, 15, mother alcohol misuser)

From the interviews, it seemed that siblings could also act as role models for survival: several of the above respondents mentioned that they themselves or a sibling had shown the way by getting out of the home and establishing an independent life for themselves. However, some of them had mixed feelings about their siblings' actions, particularly if they had rejected the parent, but still valued their example.

Wider family support – from grandparents, aunts, uncles, cousins – also varied considerably in our sample, from a few who said they had felt embedded in a large extended family to six who identified no one in their extended families to whom they had been able to turn at any time.

> And then I moved in wi' my uncle, my mum's eh little brother. And my auntie ... basically his door's always been open – open to me at any time.
> (Claire, 22, father heroin misuser)

Thirty respondents gave extensive descriptions of support from one member of their extended family, most commonly a grandmother or an aunt (whether or not a blood relative). Thirteen mentioned an aunt as having been important, one mentioned a grandfather, another an uncle and 16 mentioned grandmothers. This support seemed to be significant to them. Some of these family members had a very proactive and, in a few cases, a parental role. Two respondents' aunts had become their foster-carers, while four had lived with their grandparents at various points. Several other respondents of both genders identified an aunt as a person they could talk to.

It appeared that there might also be difficulties and risks associated with support from extended family members. Rachel (17, mother alcohol misuser) described how difficult she found it to cope with her otherwise extremely supportive grandparents because of their criticisms of her mother, whom she felt she had to defend. Extended family support could also prove fragile over time because of death, arguments, and other family pressures, including finances. Michael (19, father alcohol misuser) was angry about the decision of social services not to allow him to stay with his grandmother, because she was considered too old to look after him. Lucy (17, mother alcohol misuser) bitterly recounted how her aunt, who had called herself her mother, cut all ties when she became pregnant. She felt that this rejection made her unwilling to trust new people who came into her life. One man rejected his aunt and uncle after his aunt had told his grandparents that his mother had been put in prison:

> My uncle, aye, I used tae be close tae him when I was younger. But then I just found out that they were just so twisted and two faced.
> (Dan, 21, mother and two stepfathers heroin misusers)

In some families, the lack of extended family support was related to geographical distance or parental separation. Several respondents commented that extended family members had 'disowned' their parent(s) as a result of their substance misuse. One woman's family, for example, were angry that she and her siblings were placed with foster-parents at various times. She herself, however, did not feel that her family's reaction had helped her and her siblings, as this extract shows:

> Sarah Wilson: Are you close to your extended family?

Alexis: *Mm. Well some of them don't talk to my mum ... My mum speaks tae my nanna. And I'm close to her, but eh my mum and my uncle and my auntie don't get on. But I still speak to them. But it's kinda only when I'm at my nanna's kind o' thing.*
(Alexis, 17, mother alcohol, heroin, poppers misuser)

Supportive non-family relationships

When respondents talked about their lives, it appeared that friends and neighbours also played important roles for some of them, even though a significant minority reported difficulties in making friends until the mid-teenage years. More respondents reported having at least one 'close' friend. In a few cases, these were adult friends of their parents who were described as having played a strong advisory role. Some respondents had developed friendships with young people in similar family situations, some of whom they met through using services, including young carers organisations.

These people, and the help they offered, were important to many respondents but, again, such relationships were not without their pitfalls. In some instances, the respondents' accounts indicated that friendships had led to their engagement in shorter- or longer-term periods of self-destructive behaviour, including excess drinking, criminal activity and serious drug misuse. Six young men recounted how their heroin misuse had started through friends, whom they also described as 'family'. Four of them were still struggling with heroin addiction when interviewed.

The type of support provided by friendships also depended in part on how much friends (and their parents) knew of their family situation. Emma (21, mother alcohol misuser) was open with her friends. This was not the case for all respondents, however. Their accounts suggested that important help could be given by people who provided respite but did not intervene.

Respondents' discussions of their friendships also revealed their concerns around confiding in friends specifically, and talking about their problems in general. Friendships could offer a haven from problems, as well as escapist fun. However, disclosure about the realities of home life ran the risk of rejection. Several respondents indicated that they had not spoken about their home situation even with 'close' friends, and did not invite their friends home. Their concern was that the friendship itself would be threatened by burdening others with their problems. Although a minority did identify at least one friend in whom they had been able to confide as teenagers, these accounts still emphasised the importance of carefully managing and limiting access to knowledge of their lives.

Overall, the respondents' views on the importance of talking about problems varied. Talking or 'not bottling things up' was adopted by many older respondents as a helpful strategy, usually once they had left the family home. Even so, talking could be a strain:

[Talking] *takes a lot of me, like I say, because I've been and oot of care. I feel like I dinnae get close like even like for example my key worker.*
(Claire 22, father heroin misuser)

And for others, it simply underlined their feelings of impotence.

The idea of family

The overall picture provided by the respondents was that only a minority had any long-term, unconditionally supportive relationships. In spite of many examples of damaging experiences, the need and desire for close, family-type relationships still permeated many of these interviews, and some respondents' accounts suggested feelings of shame and embarrassment about their lack of any real family ties.

In this context, it is unsurprising that many younger respondents, in particular, appeared to have been remarkably loyal to and understanding of their substance-misusing parent, although with reservations, as noted in Chaper 2. Further, some respondents, whose parents had severe substance misuse problems, treasured the memory of fleeting periods in which their parents were sober and 'there' for them:

A couple of Christmases ago, she was sober from the 18th to the 26th ... And we went out shopping and we been skating. We done a lot within those days. But then she went back to the drink.
(Rachel, 17, mother alcohol misuser)

Another reaction to the absence of feeling cared about was the way in which several respondents spoke of people, including service providers, friends and relatives, as substitute parents or family members. This man described a cousin who was slightly older than him, as:

The sister I've never had, the dad that's never been there. The Mum that's always with someone else.
(Jeff, 16, mother alcohol misuser)

Others emphasised their closeness to often much younger (half-)siblings, nephews or nieces, and in one case two aunts, whom they seldom saw but 'loved to bits':

My two aunties are, the two aunties that I'm close to I love to bits. We just don't see each other that much.
(Jemma, 22, father heroin misuser)

The school environment

Schooling was highly disrupted for many respondents, with several only getting there under their own steam. When there, school was an environment that had both possibilities and problems for respondents. Many spoke positively about enjoying sports, dancing or other school activities. Regardless of their experiences of school per se, most, though not all, said that they appreciated the chance to be with their friends and used it as a gateway to other enjoyable activities. Some described such activities specifically as ways to get away from home. The importance of school in terms of developing friendships was highlighted by Rachel (17, mother alcohol misuser), but she also pointed to the limits placed on this respite by her home situation. Fearing her mother might injure herself, she attended school more and more rarely, losing friends whose support had been important to her.

For a minority of respondents, mostly young women, going to school every day was seen in itself as something to hang on to, offering a chance of respite from the pressures and unpredictability of home life:

> *I probably liked the – the first primary school I*
> *went in ... it was getting me out the house at the*
> *time ... I probably felt safer there than I did at*
> *home.*
> (Jemma, 22, father heroin misuser)

Other respondents, mostly young men, spoke of disliking school, of behaving badly and of being suspended or excluded. Problems mostly arose at secondary school. Several young men recalled it as a place of violence and bullying. They struggled to explain why they had found it so difficult to adapt to secondary school life, referring, perhaps somewhat formulaically, to difficulties in accepting authority. One man suggested that he used school as a place to vent his frustrations at his home situation:

> [Stepfather] *would like get tanked up with drink*
> *and he'd abuse me. Hit me. Take it oot on me and*
> *that so I would just, I would go oot, take it oot on*
> *other people I suppose.*
> (Robbie, 18, stepfather alcohol misuser)

Overall, their accounts suggested that at secondary school age, these young men found it difficult to 'leave home behind' when at school. Interestingly, two young men reported that being sent to residential schools was an entirely positive experience for them. They appreciated the smaller staff–pupil ratios, more practical subjects taught, and being able to call staff by their first names.

Accounts of teachers' support were mixed. Some respondents felt that teachers 'picked on' them when home disruption interfered with their schoolwork and respondents were nervous about teachers asking them if anything was wrong. One woman was ambivalent in this regard. On the one hand, she was annoyed with teachers for not noticing her problems, even during a short period in which she was often drunk at school. On the other, she did not trust teachers to be discreet and feared being treated differently to other students:

Sarah Wilson:	*Do you think it would a good idea for teachers to ask students about their family?*
Emma:	*Nah. Because ... it's gonna stand oot you're being treated differently and ... that can cause you problems as well. I wouldnae have wanted my teacher tae approach me and say, what's the matter wi' you? ... You know what, if they said your work's been affected, I'd just well, 'I'm tired,' or ... 'there's nothing the matter,' or whatever.* (Emma, 21, mother alcohol misuser)

Only a minority were largely positive, often about guidance[1] teachers. In practice, guidance teachers who knew of the respondents' family problems seemed to be the most supportive. Faith (19, father alcohol misuser) exceptionally idealised teachers as a group who contrasted with her family: 'They were the people I looked up to, who would do things for me.'

Others were lukewarm or dismissive of many of their teachers but could identify particular teachers who stood out as helpful or concerned for them, for example teachers who would not single them out if they were too sleepy to study, or who would defuse their aggression by inviting them to go outside for a cigarette. In several cases, respondents emphasised that these teachers did not know their family history, but recognised there was something wrong and showed them some understanding.

I never really spoke to the teachers as such but I always get the feeling that they – they knew there was something. That – that there was something no quite right or whatever.
(Jemma, 22, father heroin misuser)

As with friends and neighbours who suspected, but may not have 'known', these 'softer' types of support seemed to have been greatly appreciated.

Services and disclosure

From respondents' accounts, the intensity and duration of service use varied dramatically. These relationships and environments had to be negotiated and were seldom, if ever, unambiguously positive. Several, including some in very difficult situations, reported never having had any involvement with social workers or any other services while aged under 16. However, many others (16) did. Two, who had been in care for most of their lives, identified social workers as the most important people in their lives. Many of these 16 respondents had strong opinions as to why such relationships were fruitful or not. Most emphasised the importance of the worker taking the time to build an individual relationship with them, and were very critical of workers who pushed them to talk about their home environment, or '[try to] put words intae your mooth', as Tom and Peter (22 and 25,

fathers heroin misusers) put it.

They also highlighted the importance of an informal approach to these relationships, in particular that meetings should be organised flexibly away from social work offices, and involve enjoyable activities that the respondents would not otherwise have had a chance to discover. For some, their relationships with individual workers were so important to them that they regarded the workers as their family members, even as parents.

Overall, their comments focused more on the quality of relationships rather than pointing to the usefulness of any particular care model.

Youth cafés were appreciated by some as places in which they could choose whether or not to disclose information about their lives to workers:

Like, if I've got a problem and I'm depressed he'll [youth worker] come up and say, 'Are you alright?' 'Aye.' 'What's the matter?' And I'll say whatever it is. 'Right, do you want to talk aboot it?' 'Nah.' 'Right, bye.' That's the end of it.
(Jeff, 16, mother alcohol misuser)

In general, while still living with their parents, there seemed to be a fear among many respondents that disclosure of parental substance misuse would result in them being taken away from home. There were other dangers felt by them: several were concerned that their parent would react violently, others felt too ashamed of their parents and were concerned family problems might be their fault. For others still, any involvement with social work was seen as being shameful and possibly making things worse. Trying to keep the substance misuse secret, and seeing few options but to live with it, characterised respondents' childhoods. Those services and environments that could provide understanding without demanding disclosure of information, and which allowed the respondent to control when and to whom they disclosed information about their lives, were highly thought of.

Conclusion

What respondents could do to control or limit the impact of parental substance misuse was shaped by: age; experience; their need to care for and protect siblings; the structure and geographical distribution of their families; and the response of their parents and others. Exclusively 'protective' factors were difficult to identify: most had some element of contingency to them. The supports on which they could draw were seldom in place unconditionally. The strategies the respondents used often had

associated costs, and some were tried and abandoned in an often painful process of trial and error. Disclosure of parental substance misuse and associated problems to extended family members, and certainly to services, could be very difficult. Non-disclosure could itself be seen as a protective strategy in some cases. The support of other adults in their lives, including service providers, was also dependent on how much those adults knew about the young person's situation.

As they grew older, nearly all of the sample had left their parents' homes permanently. Some left before the age of 16 to live with relatives, including older siblings, or to go into care. Others left after the age of 16, using supported accommodation and other services to set up their own homes. The pathways to independence and adulthood are the focus of the next chapter.

4 Growing out of family substance misuse

This chapter explores the process of developing independence and what that meant for this sample of young people affected by parental substance misuse. It focuses on these young people's goals and dreams for their futures, what being a young person meant to them, what getting their life together meant, their attitudes towards and experiences of jobs, education and family formation, and the role services played in mediating important changes in their lives. Issues of choice and control are explored. The ways in which achieving independence is influenced by diverse personal experiences, gender and socio-economic context are also discussed.

Transitions

There has been much emphasis in sociological and youth studies work on the meaning and nature of transitions for young people. This has partly been driven by a recognition that rapid social and economic change has impacted on the transition to adulthood. Trajectories have become more uncertain, periods of dependency are often longer, and the whole process more diverse and risky. The persistence of inequalities and the constraints imposed by socio-economic disadvantage still influence outcomes for young people (Furlong and Cartmel, 1997), despite a growing emphasis on individual choice and opportunity.

Transitions to adulthood can be marked in a range of ways: establishing an independent home; going to college; and gaining employment. Relationships with family, friends and locality may change, ties may be severed or cemented.

However, the whole concept of transition to adulthood presupposes a period of childhood and dependency, an assumption that is not wholly appropriate for all young people in all social and familial circumstances. Some may have been carers when very young; others may not have grown up with a constant adult carer, and, as Chapter 2 highlighted, this was very much the case for our respondents. Many in this study had experienced childhoods marked by changes, early independence, responsibilities, caring for others and learning to 'get by'. Other transitions in terms of changing living arrangements and disrupted schooling also perforated many of these young people's lives.

This situation can be contrasted with the pervasive impression in British society that the period of 'youth' is being elongated. Only eight respondents still lived with one or both parents, and several felt very insecure there. Several more had living arrangements that appeared to be very precarious, for instance staying with aunts, friends or a sister, or in a boyfriend's or girlfriend's flat. Two lived in university accommodation, and another university student had her flat bought for her by relatives. Six lived in supported accommodation, which had often been gained after long periods in temporary accommodation such as bedsits. One was in a hostel and two were in SACRO[1] homes. Six had council flats.

The sample of young people in this study spoke of diverse anticipated futures, for example to get away from the area in which they were brought up, or to stay there with friends and, in many cases, family. However, the similarity of their hopes for the future was striking and familiar: a house, job and family, contrasting with the diversity of experiences on the road to achieving this.

Goals and dreams

Nearly all the respondents expressed future-oriented goals and dreams. Goals were very clearly stated by some, and clear pathways to achieving them were described, usually through education (see below). Often respondents were already on these pathways or had hopes to be so in the near future, as with this middle-class young woman:

> I'm pretty optimistic about the future. I'm looking forward to it. I mean I'm enjoying my time now, but … I'm looking forward to travelling and painting and things like that.
> (Julia, 16, mother and father alcohol misusers)

For others, the future seemed to be described in terms of hopes and dreams rather than goals, the difference being less in the content and more in the lack of any expression of concrete plans to achieve them. Occasionally, given the life situation of a respondent (for example, heavy drug misuse), such dreams seemed unachievable, or hopes unrealistic.

> Get a job, have kids, settle down in a nice house with a nice girlfriend and a nice car … go on holiday every year. That's my ideal future.
> (Graham, 18, mother dihydrocodeine user)

Despite differences in orientation towards the future, which will be returned to at the end of this chapter in a fuller discussion of issues of choice and control, there was remarkable similarity in the hopes and aspirations of most respondents in the study:

> Sarah Wilson: *So what are your hopes and plans for the future?*
>
> Rachel: *Having a family. Having a job. Or trying to get a job. And just really getting myself back up on my feet.*
> (Rachel, 17, mother alcohol misuser)

However, for a minority, the interview question asking about the future and future plans elicited a rather more negative response. For these few respondents, the future could not be entertained, perhaps because of their current situation or mental state. Dan (21, mother and two stepfathers heroin misusers), when asked where he would be five years into the future, answered that he felt he was going to be in exactly the same place as he is now, or worse: 'Ken we want tae start a family, we want to start a life.' Jeff (16, mother alcohol misuser) described his life in very negative terms, saying, 'I just cannae be bothered wi' the future. The future is too far away.'

Goals and dreams were thus shaped by experience and context. There seemed to be differences among our respondents according to their own substance misuse, gender and social class background, although the small sample size and qualitative nature of the study can only be suggestive of such differences. For example, as previously discussed, many more young men than women disliked school, and left with fewer qualifications. Drug-misusing respondents were less likely to have set out plans for their future, although some had taken steps in this direction, and drug-using men tended to express more highly idealised visions of their future lives.

Education and work

As noted above, some respondents seemed to have an orientation towards the future that was linked to specific goals, often educational. However, getting on with one's own life or getting one's life in order could also involve managing family relationships, setting up home, getting or keeping work, or kicking a drug habit or alcohol misuse.

Some clearly identified education as important in achieving their goals, and in particular achieving reasonable results in their Standard Grade[2] examinations and therefore being able to go on to college, or stay on at school. Others were returning to education after a more disrupted schooling. Kate described the importance of her schooling to her:

> Because if I hadn't went to school obviously then I wouldn't have been able tae do all the stuff that I'm doing. And then I wouldn't be able to get a job and everything.
> (Kate, 16, father alcohol misuser)

There was a picture from the interviews of a considerable sense of achievement amongst respondents who were able to go on to further or higher education, and that such a path would bring rewards in the future through better jobs and salary, as with this woman currently on an adult nursing course:

> Now I'm the happiest I've ever been in my life now ... it's been a five, five year long project getting the money and yeah, yeah, it's probably the happiest moment.
> (Jane, 19, stepfather alcohol misuser)

Receiving an education was seen by many as essential to a good future, and even some of those whose lives were very disrupted were attending college. University represented one means of setting themselves up independently, but was limited to a few. However, for others, the experience of school and exclusion from it made continuing in education more difficult or less appealing.

Although about half of the respondents were in receipt of benefits, mainly due to depression or drug misuse, some were in employment. For a few, these jobs were viewed positively, seemed to be a source of self-esteem and satisfaction, and enabled a positive outlook on the future:

> I love working. I like getting up in the morning and going to work and putting everything into my work and trying my best at it.
> (Tabetha, 17, mother alcohol misuser)

Others talked positively about future careers, particularly in the care sector, for example as social workers. Some respondents questioned this career path, wondering whether it would remind them of their parents, but a few were pursuing education to achieve this and others were involved in volunteer work.

However, work was not viewed positively by everybody, and some had poorly paid jobs with few prospects, such as in fast-food outlets. Such jobs might be filling in a gap, and providing a source of income for future aspirations, but for others, especially if no educational opportunities were available or being taken up, such jobs were seldom reported as fulfilling. Mark (16, stepfather alcohol, cousin heroin misuser) described dropping out of college despite wanting to do graphic design, 'something stopped me', then said, 'I was being a DJ and then I stopped that and now I just want to be a rap artist'. He was currently working in a fast-food outlet to save money; he had few educational qualifications and also felt that the presence of a chronic illness meant the type of job he wanted would not be open to him.

Day to day

> *Nobody's got any faith in us whatsoever, so we need tae find things tae do every day.*
> (Dan, 21, mother and two stepfathers heroin misusers)

Although many respondents seemed to talk about their futures in terms of making plans and managing their independence through education, improved relationships with their families, and living away from home, a sizeable minority seemed to be much more oriented towards getting through on a day-to-day basis, thinking in the short term. For most of these respondents, the persistence of a drug habit or, less frequently, heavy alcohol misuse seemed to overwhelm any potential for longer-term planning.

> *So obviously I'm trying tae decorate but trying tae decorate everything, moving intae a hoose and trying tae decorate a' and that when you've got a smack habit is hard. Hard work.*
> (Peter, 25, father heroin misuser)

For some, taking each day as it came itself enabled a future, and many described the need to get their own lives in order:

> Sarah Wilson: *And have things got better for you do you think?*
>
> Graham: *A wee bit aye, starting to get on my own and get my life in order.*
> (Graham, 18, mother dihydrocodeine misuser)

These strategies resonate with those described in Chapter 3, with getting by on a day-to-day basis itself being one way of dealing with adverse circumstances.

Relationship to locality and friends

Further or higher education sometimes meant respondents leaving their own locality and friends, something often perceived as a positive step towards leading their own lives. Ian (23, mother and father alcohol misusers), for example, said that moving was one of the most important influences on his life. Several respondents, particularly those who had developed heroin problems, demonstrated a strong awareness of the influence of place on their lives and the necessity of breaking bonds which they perceived as holding them in their current situation:

> *When if you spend time with people who want more out of life then you want more out of life as well.*
> (Jemma, 22, father heroin misuser)

> *But to get sorted you've got to leave your pals. And you basically have tae change the culture. Naebody wants tae move away fae the only place they ken.*
> (Tom, 22, and Peter, 25, fathers heroin misusers)

As the second of the above quotes suggests, leaving what is familiar is not always desirable or easy. Some were ambivalent about leaving home, and worried about the safety of parents and siblings who remained. However, others described being different from those around them:

I just want out of [village] [laughs]. *It's too small, I've – I've got big ambitions, I need a big place.*
(Alexis, 17, mother heroin, alcohol, poppers misuser)

For several respondents, getting away from their parents' home was a very positive step. For Nikki (19, mother amphetamines, alcohol misuser; stepfather glue misuser), leaving home was the most 'positive' action she had ever taken. Similarly, Lana (20, father alcohol misuser) said, 'Getting my own house is the best thing I've ever done', and Tabetha (17, mother alcohol misuser), 'I'm a happier person … happier. I don't cry every day like I used to'. Independence was thus highly valued, although this did not necessarily mean severing all local and family ties.

Family legacy and future

As noted in Chapter 2, family had a strong symbolic significance for respondents: many had also been active carers as children. Almost all said that they wanted children at some point in the future. Seven had children already and one was pregnant. For all these respondents, providing for their children and making sure they would have a different start in life to the one they had was described as important. However, two young men did not see their sons and this meant an 'arm's length' engagement with their children. Three others who were parents had drug problems and described their children as the main incentive for their participation in methadone maintenance programmes. Tom (22, father heroin misuser) said, 'The promises I've made my bairn. I'll be able to keep they promises when I'm on methadone.'

A very few did not want children. For example, Allan (17, mother alcohol misuser) said that he did not want a family because of the way he had been treated and because of his sister splitting up from her partner: 'It'll just be me, my sister and her bairns.'

Respondents were also asked about whether they had any worries for the future because of their parents' or other family members' substance misuse. A few responded that they did have concerns that they might turn out like their parents, siblings or other relatives, because of a family history of substance misuse or mental health problems. However, most gave a sense of having some control over this:

I think I should really like think about it, because, I mean there's been a like a chain of mental health problems in the family, sort of things like that, people burying it like because that generation they tend to bury things and didn't talk about it … Just keep on … be aware of the way you behave when you're older, because I think it's like bound to affect you, you're lucky if it doesn't. Like I've just constantly been trying to keep an eye on the way I'm going to behave because you can see the pattern of it, it's obviously like a generation thing that goes down.
(Julia, 16, mother and father alcohol misusers)

Most respondents did not report specific worries on this account, however:

Aboot drugs and alcohol? No because it's mild drugs and my granddad's cut down on the drink so it's not really a problem I'm … because I told him, 'Sort your life oot or you're no having any of us'.
(Mark, 17, grandfather alcohol misuser)

Although some saw leaving their families, and sometimes their home area, as crucial to being independent and getting on with their lives, this did not always mean a complete severing of family ties:

> *I think I'll have probably quite a good relationship with my mum. Even though I will want space.*
> (Jane, 19, stepfather alcohol misuser)

As noted in earlier chapters, family seemed to remain important for most respondents. Hopes for future good relationships were often expressed in the interviews, although these were sometimes talked about forlornly:

> *We used to be a really, really, really close family but it's all like shifted really. But hopefully we'll get there … some day.*
> (Lana, 20, father alcohol misuser)

The role of services

> *Leaving care services, em kinda I'm too old for their help now. Em, but when I came back up … and ended up homeless and helping out here. [S] who works here really helped me. She has been really important in loads of ways. She's a support worker here and she's – she's really helped me a lot. It was her that got, referred me to the place that I'm staying in because I was made homeless while I was doing things for here … [she] is more down to earth, younger.*
> (Jemma, 22, father heroin misuser)

Services were described as playing an important role in aiding the respondents' transition to independent living. Thirteen respondents had sought help with drug or alcohol problems. Several also received support for mental health problems including depression, anorexia,

anxiety and stress. Three of the eight respondents who reported having depression had community psychiatric nurses and were very positive about them.

Several respondents who had left home had done so, and been supported in their new homes, with the help of various services. Eight were housed by supported accommodation services and the key workers who formed an integral part of these services were described as very important to them. These services helped respondents to cope with bills, to cook for themselves, and with other life skills. Several also emphasised the importance of being able to 'drop in' on voluntary sector agencies for chats and advice during this potentially lonely period in their new home:

> *Because, eh, it was like, it was somewhere I used to go every day. And eh I would sit down and talk to them and take me for a game of pool or whatever. And they got my college course. They got that set up for me.*
> (Robbie, 18, stepfather alcohol misuser)

Most said that they had to wait for significant periods before they could obtain supported accommodation. Several described living in various types of hostels and other homelessness accommodation before being rehoused. This was often a difficult period for them.

Robbie was ecstatic about his new flat, explaining:

> *I've got my own space, and no one around, em, no one banging on my door like at the hostel, asking me if I want drugs … So I can sit in my flat and no one can come in and pester me.*

Access to supported accommodation was generally obtained through social workers or voluntary agencies. Many respondents did not know about these services and had little help with setting themselves up in council flats. For instance, Jeff (16, mother alcohol misuser) depended on money from his grandparents.

In talking about their move to independence, respondents had strong opinions on what had and had not worked for them, and what services might be useful for others. They talked about a variety of services they would like, but opinion was divided in the sample as a whole. For instance, many thought support groups composed of others in similar circumstances would be helpful, but some just as strongly desired individual counselling and felt groups would not work for them. Only one had been through family therapy, which she thought was worthwhile. Other respondents were ambivalent at this suggestion, one not wanting to talk in front of his parents, while others were aware of resistance on the part of parents to acknowledging that there was a problem.

Youth groups were mentioned positively, especially if located in the city centre where they could be easily accessed. An advocate was recommended by some, someone to talk to and whom they could build a relationship with, preferably without their parents knowing. Despite wariness of social workers among some, with hindsight others thought that social workers should be more proactive in removing children from substance-using parents. There was also some interest in services for the substance-using parent. Reflecting on his own past, Paul (25, stepmother and two foster-fathers alcohol misusers) stated that there was a need for drug education for people in foster care.

Breaking free or carefree?

As noted above, many of the young people described the need to leave their own friends and neighbourhood, and also to break free from their families. Some described themselves as being mature, and that their experiences as children made them know what life was like. For example, Sean (17, father cannabis misuser) said that he felt that he had more experience and was more independent than others his age because he moved out from his mother's house at age 11. This woman expressed similar sentiments in relation to independence:

> I mean I'm 17 but, well, I ken myself, but folk also tell me that I'm so grown up. And that's because, well, I've had tae basically look after myself my whole life.
> (Lucy, 17, mother alcohol misuser)

For some of these young people, transitions in the teenage years involved moving from responsibilities as carers to being real teenagers and 'getting a life' in terms of having fun and not having to look after others.

> I want to try and make something of my life because when I was young I never got that.
> (Faith, 19, father alcohol misuser)

Although those expressing these views were a minority, they shed an interesting light on the assumptions underpinning the transition to adulthood as being one of increased responsibility and independence. Independence for some in this study was valued for the decrease in responsibilities it could bring.

Choice and control

Although a sense of agency and resilience was present in many of the young people's accounts, this was not the case across the board. The interview accounts presented a serious challenge to the notion of choice in relation to youth transitions, and demonstrate the presence of very real constraints in terms of lack of education for some, criminal convictions or pending sentences for others, lack of a home or employment, a substance misuse problem, or continued difficult relationships with family. However, to suggest that such constraints always overwhelmed an individual's ability to confront and change his or her environment is to underestimate the drive of some of these young people. The continued influence of socio-economic advantage, despite being in a family affected by drug or alcohol misuse, was also evident, as some had greater resources, especially material, to support independence.

In terms of issues relating to agency and resilience, respondents' accounts were different in terms of apparent degree of control or sense of control over the future. Some seemed to have a clear sense of their own control and that this could be described in terms of goals and plans and getting on with it. For others, there was not such a sense of control: their hopes for the future might be similar, but it seemed to be perceived as a question of luck or chance whether or not these hopes would be realised.

For those respondents whose accounts evoked a sense of some control and choice, how they spoke about the future seemed to comprise a sense of both changing and influencing what happens and adapting or responding to what is thrown at them.

Then I suppose I came to a point when I thought, 'This isn't going to get me naewhere in life', sort of thing. And stuck my heid down I suppose. Nothing will stop me. Whether it'll take me ten years, I'll still dae it. I've got three Highers, I could go straight to university but I think I'll go to college first, ken. Got an A for English and a B for Maths and an A for admin so ... Nine months pregnant I done my exams.
(Lucy, 17, mother alcohol misuser)

Some described control over their own behaviour as a way of preventing themselves becoming like the using parent:

It worries me because sometimes I think, 'What if I turn out like my mum? What if I treat my kids like the way my mum has?' It just goes through my mind every now and then. But I realise I can do it, I don't need to go in my mum's footsteps. I can dae it myself ... I think it would make it a bit easier because I know now what to expect. Even though I'm not going to turn out a raging alcoholic [laughs], you know, it's like I know, I know what to expect.
(Rachel, 17, mother alcohol misuser)

For others, their accounts in the interviews suggested less control, more ambivalence about the future, within an overall optimistic context:

Just hope I stick into college and get a, get myself a good job once I've finished the course ... I feel more positive than negative.
(Jeff, 16, mother alcohol misuser)

For a few, there was even less sense of control and the future seemed less optimistic:

I feel like I'm stuck in a rut ... I dunno, so many paths that are open to me I don't know what

ones I want to go down, I've already been down the bad path.
(Stuart, 19, mother cannabis misuser)

Of course, respondents could express optimism and pessimism in the same interview, and this woman, despite saying that she felt in control of her life, also remarked:

I always say, 'What's the point of looking to the future, because you cannae choose what's gonnae happen'.
(Faith, 19, father alcohol misuser)

Growing out of parental substance misuse for these young people was obviously hard; taken-for-granted elements in the transition to adulthood were not necessarily present. Some had to be independent from a very early age, as carers themselves or due to lack of parental care, throwing into question the very usefulness of the term 'transition' to describe the trajectories of these young people as they moved towards adulthood. Breaking ties with the past in order to establish a future seemed to be important, although such ties may be recreated from a position of independent living:

The most difficult thing is trying tae separate myself fae what I had then. To try and get a new life now. That's the difficult thing ... I've got to break away, I've got to break the chains ... I hope it's gonna be a good future. But then there's the fear it might all just collapse around me. Because I could lose my mum for good and I don't want that.
(Rachel, 17, mother alcohol misuser)

And past experience could lead even the most pessimistic to suggest optimism about the future:

It cannae get any worse eh?
(Michael, 19, father alcohol misuser)

Conclusion

This chapter has examined respondents' accounts of where they were and where they wished to be in the context of developing independence. Respondents were in what is usually considered to be a time of transition from childhood and adolescence to adulthood. Yet their experiences confound notions of childhood as a time of dependence and lack of responsibility, and adulthood as a time of independence and responsibility. Some were experiencing for the first time the chance to put their needs and desires to the fore. All had strong ideals about their preferred futures – to have a job, family and house. Some had made careful plans to achieve their goals. Educational attainment seemed to be strongly related to positive futures in terms of achieving independent living and the prospect of good employment. For others, their ideal future seemed to be more of a dream as they struggled with the day-to-day challenges of getting by or getting their lives in order. Independence seldom meant complete rejection of their families, but offered the possibility of renewed relationships at a distance. Services were described as having a role to play both in helping respondents live and cope day to day and in working out plans for the future.

5 Discussion and conclusion

Introduction

There are increasing numbers of children growing up in families affected by substance misuse. Alcohol misuse continues to have high prevalence and drug misuse continues to rise, to the extent that services are now sometimes dealing with three affected generations. There is increasing concern among policy makers and service providers about the short- and long-term effect of parental substance misuse on children, and about ways in which these problems might be tackled so that the impact on them can be minimised. Growing policy interest is underscored by the publication of *Hidden Harm* (Advisory Council on the Misuse of Drugs, 2003) and *Getting Our Priorities Right* (Scottish Executive, 2003). Research in this area is also expanding, focusing on the impact on children (Hogan, 1998; Barnard and McKeganey, 2004) and the continued legacy borne into adulthood (Velleman and Orford, 1999), the latter being an area perhaps less well covered by policy and practice. Older children of substance-misusing parents, the focus of this study, are a group requiring support, who are relatively neglected by services and are a largely hidden population. This chapter will summarise the main issues raised in this report before going on to discuss their implications for policy, practice and further research.

The findings from this study both reinforce and expand current knowledge as well as providing some new and more detailed insights into the experiences of young people affected by parental substance misuse. These can be broadly embraced within the twin themes of resilience and transition: in other words, getting by in and getting out of, as well as growing up in and growing out of, parental substance misuse. In research and practice there is a developing interest in processes of resilience in children and young people. Our focus is on the capacity of young people to function in adversity. In the accounts of their childhoods the young people in this study told us how they 'got by' when living with parental substance misuse. Resilience can also mean the capacity to move beyond those adverse circumstances, and we also examined what the young people told us about 'moving out' or moving on, setting this in the context of transitions to adulthood. Through this conceptual approach, we hope to have demonstrated the agency displayed by the young people interviewed without reifying their capabilities; as the many illustrations in the report indicate, the nature of the adversity they faced was both harrowing and, often, overwhelming. The complexity of their experiences, and their own and others' reactions to it, can emerge from the rich data generated through first-hand accounts. Understanding that complexity is essential to sensitive policy making and practice.

This study involved 38 young people, men and women, aged 15–27, from diverse circumstances. It explored their experiences of parental substance misuse, whether drugs or alcohol or both, through the use of qualitative research methods. The young people were asked to reflect on their childhoods; discuss their current situation; and anticipate their futures. Specific research tools – a life grid and in-depth, open-ended interviewing – were used to promote a strongly biographical account grounded in the young person's own perspectives and reports of their life. This overall focus on young people's own experience and our analysis of it led to three key research questions: what problems does parental substance misuse cause? What helps young people get through these experiences? What can be done by services to help?

What the young people told us about ...

What problems does parental substance misuse cause?

No reader can fail to be moved by the accounts of the young people who participated in this study; the harshness of their experience is illustrated in their stark expressions:

> *... well I've basically had tae look after myself my whole life.*
> (Lucy, 17, mother alcohol misuser)

> *It was the most hellish experience that you could ever imagine.*
> (Ian, 23, both parents alcohol misusers)

> *Eleven or twelve ... That's when, that's when things went sshhh, doonhill for me eh.*

> Sarah Wilson: *And why was that? Why did they go downhill?*

> *Because I wasnae getting put to high school. I wasnae going, I wasnae getting put tae school. My ma's going oot working in the fields. Coming hame tae every c... lying wrecked ken all my da's mates lying wrecked aboot the hoose.*
> (Tom, 22, and Peter, 25, fathers heroin misusers)

As in other studies, this research identified disruption, neglect, unpredictability and violence among the harms related to parental substance misuse, as the respondents described their lives. Substance misuse was, of course, central to their experiences, but not in isolation – violence and mental health problems were also common, and sexual abuse was experienced by a few. Most of the sample also came from deprived backgrounds, with resources sometimes even more diminished by a parent's illegal substance misuse.

However, this reality was also a taken-for-granted aspect of their lives and the respondents' modes of expression sometimes seemed to understate the risk, disruption and damage their family life (or lack of it) was causing. Their accounts of their childhood revealed a growing awareness of parental substance misuse, the experience of felt or potential stigma this brought, and the need to manage information and the complex relationships within the family and beyond. Hiding parental substance misuse as well as hiding from it indeed suggests a 'hidden harm'.

The young people talked about how they themselves cared about and for their families, and how they were cared about and cared for themselves (albeit intermittently) by a range of family members and others, including service providers. About half the sample described themselves as having been active carers as children, looking after the practical and emotional needs of a parent or siblings. This enabled their basic needs to be met (cooking food, cleaning the home, washing clothes) and sometimes protected them from immediate danger (calling on neighbours or extended family members for help), as well as ensuring the safety of the substance-misusing parent (by making sure they did not harm themselves when drunk or high). Such role reversal not only added a further complexity to family relationships, especially if the parent became capable again from time to time, but was also sometimes described as a source of self-esteem and maturity.

The gendered nature of care was evident in the respondents' accounts: more young women than men reported that they had been carers as children, and respondents also talked about maternal substance misuse in a way that suggests specific gendered expectations around parenting. There seemed to be lower expectations around fathering than mothering, and greater feelings of being let down by a mother's perceived failure to care for or care about them. The interview accounts also suggested that a non-using parent was not necessarily a support or ally in difficult family circumstances. The dynamics of care sometimes made the process of leaving home even more difficult for some.

Realisation of parental substance misuse brought with it a sense that their experience was not normal. This sometimes found expression in the interviews when respondents poignantly described 'normal' or 'happy' times, perhaps when a parent was dry for a period of time, or when celebrations or a family outing occurred without disruption or embarrassment. Their families, although frequently described in ways that suggest a damaged and damaging entity, were of central importance to many of these young people. They had to grapple with the complex emotions of anger, pity and love, in the knowledge that their parent, although felt to care about them, was not able to care for them. The preservation of a sense of family permeated much of what the young people said. A sense of an idealised family emerged, with a desire for closeness and uncomplicated and unconditional love. Maintaining some sense of family, while experiencing its lack on a daily basis, seemed to

lead some to offer accounts which could themselves be interpreted as protective. Lower expectations of parenting or family life, memories of infrequent happy times, not being let down by no longer expecting abstinence, not placing trust in relationships, were all described in the interviews.

A large minority of the sample had a current or past drug problem, although most did not and many had a strong sense of wanting to avoid the problems they had observed being caused by their parents' substance misuse. Some had gone through periods of heavy drug use in the past, but had stopped by the time of interview. Others were in a treatment programme. The accounts we collected suggest that peer and environmental influences, and exposure to different kinds of drug use in the home, seemed to be linked to respondents' routes into drug use, although evidence of a direct relationship between parent and child use was mixed. Rather, there were vulnerabilities and exposures in some respondents' lives that made them susceptible to problem drug use, which itself then became a source of vulnerability for them.

Building an independent life was no easy trajectory for most of these young people, and their accounts suggest no sense of a gradual transition to adulthood. Many had experienced a foreshortened childhood, through the taking on of caring responsibilities and learning to look after themselves. Role reversal between parent and child itself was sometimes described as making the transition to independent living difficult, as concern was still felt for the parent left behind. For a few, growing independence actually seemed to offer the chance to be free of responsibilities for the first time. The respondents also described childhoods pervaded by transitions and changes. Disrupted home life, continued concern for a parent or sibling, disrupted schooling, their own drug use, all made living independently post 16 no easy option.

What helps them get through these experiences?

The young people described the different ways in which they protected themselves and others while growing up with parental substance misuse. Invoking some sense of control over their environment seemed to be important, especially since direct challenges to their parents' behaviour were reported as being both futile and counterproductive: it could lead to a worsening of the situation, for example through increased violence. More subtle forms of control were reported, for example removing oneself, and sometimes one's siblings, into the privacy and protection of their own room. Crying on one's own, literally staying out of harm's way, turning up music to cover up noise or tidying up were all described as ways of minimising the impact of parental substance misuse. When older, some described the unobtrusive respite a friend's home might provide. As noted above, many talked as if they made do with symbolic care (being cared about rather than cared for), although for some even this was absent. A few described how they or a sibling had rejected a parent, which could be interpreted as an ultimate strategy of control.

The respondents described a range of other factors that helped them get through these experiences, in addition to their own day-to-day and longer-term actions. Most had some kind of support from an extended family member (most often a grandmother or aunt), sometimes formalised in fostering. However, although characterised as important, these relationships also seemed fragile in a range of ways: there was always a possibility of rejection or other kinds of dissolution of the relationship. For most respondents, such relationships never seemed unconditional, but were part of a complex web of contingent emotional ties. Friendships, too, were often described as important and supportive; such friendships could provide a haven or respite, or simply be fun. However, such relationships also involved the need to manage information about parental substance misuse, and there was often a fear of rejection that any revelation might incur. Non-disclosure might be usefully characterised as a protective strategy.

The young people also talked about the ways in which they hoped to reach their goals and dreams of having a house, job and family. For some, active planning seemed to have placed them well on the way to this, most often through continued education to secure a better job. However, this was much less likely to be the case for those facing their own problematic substance misuse. For them, getting their lives together seemed to be more focused on the day to day, rather than the longer term. Sometimes, leaving their neighbourhood and setting up an independent home was described as an important way out of their past experience and a route to independence. Some expressed a sense of control over their futures, others less so. Resilience, then, can perhaps be described as an ability both to change and influence what happens to you and to respond effectively to what life throws at you.

What can be done by services to help?

A wider context of potential support was also referred to when respondents also described their schooling and other services. However, the picture to emerge was not one of holistic or integrated support for their needs. School was experienced as positive by some, providing relief from home, but as negative by others, who seemed to reject school or be rejected by it. Teachers' roles were often described in ambivalent ways: some had been supportive, but others had not. The respondents' accounts suggest that there are inherent difficulties here; some support seemed to be needed, but it could not be overtly given or be too interventionist in nature. Issues of the control of information and concern about the possible negative impact of revelations about one's family circumstances form both the context for and constraints around support. In relation to other services, for those who had experienced social work involvement, it seemed to be the quality of the relationship that was important, and the extent to which the support did not result in direct intervention in the home environment. In relation to living an independent life, respondents described some service support as helpful, especially the more informal youth services. Support workers in relation to supported accommodation also seemed to help.

Implications for policy and practice

We have here a group of young people requiring different kinds and levels of support, but who are somewhat neglected by services and are a rather hidden population. They and their accounts need to be part of the debate about substance misuse. Awareness across all

agencies of the hidden nature of their need, itself exacerbated by their own actions in terms of isolation and fear of disclosure, will be important. A holistic and integrated approach to policy must be developed, not just for very young children, but right through to young adulthood and beyond. However, such integration must foreground the young people's own needs and views, with sensitive reaction to their desire for privacy; recognition of the continued importance of family ties; recognition of their own agency; and unobtrusive support provided in a non-stigmatising way. The ways in which these young people themselves manage to get by and get through their experiences must be supported. Particular attention must be paid to the isolation that some of their forms of management might bring, and also to the positive ways in which many tried to build an independent life as they moved into young adulthood.

The importance of wider kin must also be recognised by services, although the possibility that they too may have a substance misuse problem needs to be acknowledged. These relationships, experienced as helpful by the young people in this study, could be supported and perhaps made less contingent and conditional. It is also important that services foster ways to support continued ties with a parent or parent figure, where this is desired by the young person, while at the same time supporting the young person in independent living. Expanded support for young carers, especially those hidden from view, is required. Young carers groups were very much appreciated by those who used them, especially as they were among the few services to offer support beyond the age of 16. Such emphasis on young carers needs to be balanced with support for using and non-using parents in their parental roles. However, assumptions must not be made about the support a non-using parent might be able to provide, as this study suggested that such support was not always available. Many respondents valued a less formal youth work approach. The profile of these services, especially their role in supporting transitions, could be enhanced.

This study can only make tentative conclusions about the extent to which these young people's experiences, and their ability to work through the impact of these, are shaped by gender and social class. However, caring is a gendered experience, and the young women also seemed to be more likely to achieve within the education system. Those few with more material resources were also better able to become independent, for example through financial help with accommodation. Since education seemed to be so closely linked to achieving goals of independence, efforts could also be made to provide alternatives to school for some.

It is also only possible to make tentative conclusions about any differences between alcohol and drug use. Overall there was similarity of experience, but some daily differences due in part to the effects of these different substances, their diverse cultural contexts, and their different legal statuses. Services need to be able to respond to this diversity as well as the range of issues, including violence, that young people affected by parental substance abuse have to face.

The effects of parental substance misuse on children and young people is clearly a cross-cutting policy issue; the often hidden nature of the problem and the ways in which children and young people deal with it pose particular challenges to policy makers, service planners and providers. This research focused directly on the accounts of young people themselves and has identified many ways in which they managed to get by and get on. However, these processes, which may develop resilience in some, are highly contingent and fragile, and may not militate against either long-term or short-term harm. Working to support young people and maximising the resources they can draw on requires a policy response that operates at the level of the child, family, wider kin and community, and stretches from childhood to adulthood if harm and poor outcomes are to be ameliorated and prevented.

Notes

Chapter 1

1 'Substance misuse' refers to misuse of alcohol and illegal and prescription drugs.

2 NVivo is a software package designed to assist in the analysis of qualitative data.

3 We defined their parents as middle class when one or both were in professional/managerial-level occupations.

4 Detained under the provisions of the Mental Health Act 1983.

5 The term 'parent' is used broadly to refer to any individual who was in a parental role for a significant period of time in the respondent's life. For the purposes of this section, 'father' and 'mother' include step-parents.

Chapter 3

1 In the Scottish education system guidance teachers provide counselling and personal guidance for pupils.

Chapter 4

1 Scottish Association for the Care and Resettlement of Offenders.

2 General Certificate of Secondary Education (GCSE) equivalent.

References

Advisory Council on the Misuse of Drugs (2003) *Hidden Harm: Responding to the Needs of Children of Problem Drug Users*. London: Home Office

Alcohol Concern (2000) *Britain's Ruin*. London: Alcohol Concern

Barnard, M. and McKeganey, N. (2004) 'The impact of parental problem drug use in children: what is the problem and what can be done to help?', *Addiction*, Vol. 99, No. 5, pp. 552–9

Cuijpers, P., Langendoen, Y. and Bijl, R. (1999) 'Psychiatric disorders in adult children of problem drinkers: prevalence, first onset and comparison with other risk factors', *Addiction*, Vol. 94, No. 10, pp. 1489–98

Furlong, A. and Cartmel, F. (1997) *Young People and Social Change: Individuation and Risk in Late Modernity*. Buckingham: Open University Press

Gilligan, R. (2001) *Promoting Resilience: A Resource Guide on Working with Children in the Care System*. London: British Agencies for Adoption and Fostering

Gilligan, R. (2003) *Promoting Children's Resilience: Some Reflections*. Glasgow: Centre for the Child and Society

Hogan, D. (1998) 'The psychological development and welfare of children of opiate and cocaine users: review and research needs', *Journal of Child Psychology and Psychiatry*, Vol. 39, pp. 609–20

Scottish Executive (2003) *Getting Our Priorities Right – Policy and Practice Guidelines for Working with Children and Families Affected by Problem Drug Use*. Edinburgh: The Stationery Office

Velleman, R. and Orford, J. (1999) *Risk & Resilience: Adults Who Were the Children of Problem Drinkers*. London: Harwood